Truly Foul & Cheesy™

Scotland Facts

& Jokes

This Truly Foul & Cheesy
book belongs to:

....

Written by

John Townsend

Illustrated by

David Antram

BOOK HOUSE
a SALARIYA *imprint*

Truly Foul & Cheesy **Scotland** Facts & Jokes

Introduction

The author really hasn't made anything up in this book (apart from some daft limericks and jokes). He checked out the foul facts as best he could and even double-checked the fouler bits to make sure – so please don't get too upset if you find out something different or meet a Scottish genius, a talking haggis or a wee beastie in frilly tartan pants.

If I had my way, I'd RATify the lot!

5

Official Warning

This book contains all sorts of weird, wacky, barmy and yucky snippets about Scotland. Just like a haggis, it is packed with ingredients that some might find revolting and others might find delicious. Not all the facts are foul, as Scotland is full of fascinating places, people and events. Don't be disappointed if some of your favourite Scottish stories are missing – there are just too many to include in a little book. So, just like that haggis, all kinds of spicy bits and pieces have been mixed up here – and you might need a strong stomach to cope with it all. (Yes, stomachs and haggis go hand-in-glove as you'll soon find out).

So, puff up the bagpipes, fasten the kilt, hold on to your tam o' shanter and enjoy the ride...

Just in case you're wondering what the title of this book would be in Scottish Gaelic, try this: Scéalta agus fíricí fíor-bhréagacha agus olc na hAlban (you can put your teeth back in now). If you didn't know, Alba is Gaelic for Scotland.

Cheesy Limerick

This book is packed full of
things Scottish,
With facts; from quite
warmish to hottish.
You might laugh and howl
When the facts become foul,
But we hope that you'll
learn quite a lot-ish!

3 Scottish riddles

Q: What do you call a Scotsman with a castle on his head?
A: Fort William.

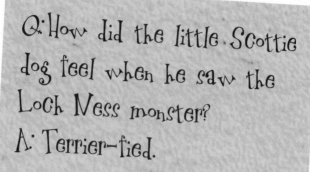

Q: How did the little Scottie dog feel when he saw the Loch Ness monster?
A: Terrier-fied.

Q: What is the name of a Scottish cloak room attendant?
A: Willie Angus McCoatup.

Don't worry… the jokes might get better (but not much).

3

RANDOM FACTS

you might not know...

1 Less than a quarter of Scotland's 790 islands are lived on by people.

2 The 5,000-year-old Fortingall Yew Tree in Perthshire is the oldest living thing in Europe.

3 Bagpipes aren't truly Scottish. They were invented in Asia and brought to Europe by the Romans. The kilt didn't start off in Scotland either. It was first worn by the ancient Egyptians as part of the Assyrian soldiers' uniform.

A quick romp through Scottish History...

Keep ooooot!

As far as we know, the first people to arrive in the north of Scotland, somewhere between 800 BC and 1000 BC, were the Picts. These ancient people were hunter-gatherers (so they must have PICT lots of berries).
The Celts came next, who probably ate wild garlic. That means they spoke Garlic Gaelic!

Vikings from Norway conquered many of Scotland's smaller islands in the 11th century before taking on the rest of Britain. The Vikings were known for being scary in battle, but were themselves scared of Scotland. A Norse document from the 1200s described Scotland as dark and dangerous, its language as impossible to understand and the people as violent and terrifying. Vikings also feared the seas around Scotland and the terrible weather.

Words that come from Old Norse are still in use in Scots language, such as 'muckle', which means large, and even 'kilt', which comes from the Old Norse word 'kjalta'.

Many a mickle maks a muckle*

*Many a penny makes a pound.

The 'redhead gene' may well have arrived in Scotland with the Vikings. Did you know Scotland has the highest percentage of people with red hair in the world? Apparently in Edinburgh 40% of people carry the 'redhead gene'. It's the world's redheaded capital.

I approach these facts gingerly

Loopy Limericks

A redheaded Scotsman named Fisher
Gingerly fished in a fissure.
But a huge salmon's fin
Knocked the fisherman in...
Now they're fishing the fissure for Fisher.

A man from the Mull of Kintyre
Went to kirk to sing in the choir
He caused quite a scandal
When he stood by a candle
And his socks, kilt and sporran
caught fire.
(There was nothing to do
but perspire!)

He ended up as a redhead
— no hair, just a red head.

3 Scottish Teasers

Q: A large aircraft with 500 people on board flies from Scotland to England.
It crashes exactly on the border between the two countries. So, where should the survivors be buried – England or Scotland?

A: Where should the 'SURVIVORS' be buried? Who buries living people? Doh!

Q: Before Ben Nevis was measured at 1,345 metres, what was the highest mountain in the British Isles?

A: It was still Ben Nevis (Tee hee)

If you can see Ben Nevis, it's about to rain. If you can't see Ben Nevis, it's raining already.

Q: Two hikers went hiking through the Scottish Grampian Mountains, without sleep for seven days. They didn't get tired – why?
A: They slept at night (groan)

19

Try your hand at these
SCOTTISH TONGUE TWISTERS:

1 Lang may your lum reek.

Rough translation – 'Long may your chimney smoke' or as a Hogmanay greeting 'May you never be without fuel for your fire.'

2 It's a braw bricht moonlicht nicht the nicht.

Rough translation – 'It's a lovely moonlit night tonight.'

3 Mony a mickle maks a muckle.

'Many a penny makes a pound.'

20

AAAAAAAAAAHHHH

4 The Leith police dismisseth us

5 A tongue twister for sports announcers was at Station Park in 1964 during a Scottish Second Division match: Forfar 5, East Fife 4

(Try saying it 5 times fast!)

How's this for a Scottish football headline to sing?

When Inverness Caledonian Thistle surprisingly beat Celtic in the Scottish Cup at Parkhead in 2000, *The Sun* newspaper was inspired by none other than *Mary Poppins*:

'Super Caley go ballistic, Celtic are atrocious!'

Thistle show 'em!

Food for thought

Centuries ago, Scottish people ate stews, broths, soups, haggis, fish and porridge. Many still do – and that's just for breakfast! But other food might come to mind when you hear of 'Scottish food'. Shortbread? Smoked salmon? Kippers? Oh and er… deep-fried Mars Bars…

Yes, many Scottish chip shops offer a service where you take in a chocolate bar of your choice (even a Creme Egg) – and they'll deep fry it in batter for that perfect heart attack treat. The deep-fried Mars Bar has become so famous that it is slowly starting to spread – just like some waistlines. Tasty, maybe – but you might need a strong (and probably expanding) stomach and a sweet tooth to like this food.

PLEASE NOTE:
not part of your 'five-a-day'.

OR,

IF YOU PREFER ANOTHER FAMOUS SCOTTISH DELICACY...

Take a pizza. Dip it in a deep fat fryer. Bring it out, dripping in fat. Yum. Foul or fab? Some Scots love them. Maybe more to your taste are neeps and tatties. A neep is simply a turnip and a tattie is – yes, you've guessed – a potato. Neeps and tatties have long been a standard part of many a Scottish meal, even with a macaroni cheese pie or the famous haggis.

How would you like to eat mashed-up sheep's innards? Yes, that's haggis. Even the famous Scottish poet Robert Burns described haggis as 'gushing entrails' – and he was trying to be kind about it. Haggis is a bit like a giant sausage balloon cooked in a sheep's stomach. It's filled with oatmeal, fat, a sheep's cut-up liver, heart, lungs, kidneys and any other gooey innards available. After it's simmered for four hours, serve up and enjoy (or not!).

English boy: What does haggis taste like?

Scottish girl: Och, it's really offal.

(In case you didn't know, offal is food made from the entrails and internal organs of an animal).

10 Tasty Haggis Facts

Ewe must be joking

1 In 1984 the first vegan-friendly haggis was launched. No sheep involved.

Until the 18th century, haggis was eaten mainly in England. Norway's version of haggis is vegetarian and is made from beans and lentils. Apparently, the first mention of a Scottish haggis wasn't until 1747.

 In fact, the most haggis today is sold in England and not Scotland. One haggis company sends 60% of the over 1,000 tons of haggis it makes to London each year.

 Importing haggis to the USA was made illegal in 1971. Could it be a secret weapon?

5 In 2003, a study revealed that up to a third of American visitors to Scotland thought a haggis was an actual animal. Can you imagine a field of grazing haggises?

I prefer RATatouille

6 Brace yourself…
you can buy haggis
flavoured crisps and
ice cream. Yum.

7 The world's biggest haggis
was made by Halls of
Scotland and weighs 2,226
lb 10 oz – that's as much
as a small car. And for
pudding? A fried Mars Bar,
of course!

8 Even though haggis is the national dish of Scotland, it wasn't invented by the Scots. It was probably invented by the Romans, who brought it to Britain over 2,000 years ago (that's a very old haggis).

Haggis with spaghetti is delectamenti!

Beware of low-flying haggis

9 Haggis hurling is an actual sport. In 2011, Lorne Coltart set the record, hurling his haggis over 66 metres. He obviously wanted to get rid of it.

10 Ireland, France, Spain and Hong Kong are the biggest buyers of haggis outside the UK. Not many people know that.

Silly Limerick

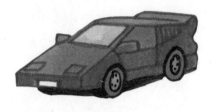

A haggis, enormous and green,
Escaped from a Clydeside canteen.
It drove through the Glens
In a Mercedes Benz
Then burst just outside Aberdeen.

SAORSA ('Freedom' in Gaelic)

Trouble with the Neighbours

For centuries there were fierce battles between Scotland and its neighbour in the south, England. Scots were fed up being ruled by Sassenachs (Gaelic for Lowlander). Over 700 years ago, William Wallace led a Scottish rebellion against Edward I of England and defeated the English army at Stirling Bridge. He is still remembered as a national hero.

William Wallace

1270-1305

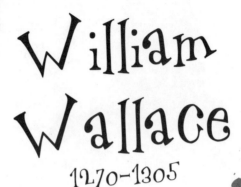

In 1298 (a year after the Stirling Bridge Battle), the Scottish and English armies fought again and this time the Scots were defeated. Wallace then went to France, to get support from the French. While he was away, Robert the Bruce made a truce with England (maybe he wanted to be called Robert the Truce instead). Edward l, the English king, offered a big reward to anyone who caught William Wallace.

Now back in Scotland, Wallace was soon to be in five places at the same time (yes, it gets messy). In 1305 he was captured and taken to London. He was charged with treason and publicly executed, being hung, drawn and quartered. His head was spiked on London Bridge and his limbs displayed in Newcastle, Berwick, Stirling and Perth. Yes, even though William Wallace was a brave hero, in the end he completely went to pieces.

Have you ever had one of those days?

Robert The Bruce
1274–1329

King Robert I of Scotland, known as Robert the Bruce, finally won Scotland's independence from England. He was descended from a French knight, Robert de Bruce, who came to England when the Normans invaded with William the Conqueror. But Robert almost gave up the struggle. Was Scotland's freedom worth the hassle?

The story goes that while he was sheltering in a hut, Robert lay on a straw bed in deep thought when a spider dangled in front of him. The spider kept trying to swing on its thread up to a beam, failing every time. Six times the spider tried and failed. 'Six times', thought Robert to himself, 'I have fought against the English and failed. If this spider fails again, I too shall give up the fight for Scotland. But if it succeeds, I shall try again.'

You can find out more on my WEBsite

The spider swung again and finally succeeded. Robert was now inspired to continue his fight against the English. He finally defeated his enemy and drove the English out of Scotland in 1314, at the Battle of Bannockburn. Phew.

Who was the famous Scot
who fell out of a fir tree?
Robert the Spruce

Who was the famous Scot who
laid an egg?
Robert the Goose

Who was the famous Scot who
sat on an orange?
Robert the Juice

Who was the famous Scot
who kept losing his pants?
Robert the Loose

Who was the famous Scottish hangman?
Robert the Noose

I've just read
the terrible noose about
the hangman

Another dip into Scottish History

Just in case someone tells you off for reading a book of silly nonsense, here are some SERIOUS FACTS with DATES so you can pretend you're doing some PROPER Scottish History. It might seem BORING – but impressive if you can slip a few details into a conversation in the middle of McDonalds... (No, not a Scottish King of Hamburgers)

Scottish Kings and Queens
House of Stewart

Name	Length of reign	Death
Robert II	(1371–1390)	illness, aged 74
Robert III	(1390–1406)	natural causes, aged 68
James I	(1406–1437)	assassinated
James II	(1437–1460)	exploding cannon
James III	(1460–1488)	killed in battle
James IV	(1488–1513)	killed in battle
James V	(1513–1542)	'nervous breakdown'
Mary I	(1542–1587)	executed
James VI	(1587–1625)	(James I of England when Scottish & English Crowns united from 1603)

41

Foul Felony

Ruling Scotland was never easy. Enemies were everywhere – both English and Scottish. Look away now if you don't want to know about the grisly end of James I of Scotland. He was a colourful king – a poet, a sportsman and musician (not necessarily all at once).

> We pirates handed over young James to King Henry IV of England, oooh aaaarrrgh

He survived being kidnapped by pirates when he was 12 years old – and the following 18 years he was a prisoner of the English.

In 1424, James made a triumphant return to Scotland but 13 years later he was brutally stabbed to death, his body dumped in a sewer below the Blackfriars monastery in Perth.

You want to know the grisly details? James I was in his royal apartment when a gang broke in to get him. He had just enough time to hide in a smelly sewer tunnel, but his exit was blocked and he was trapped and stabbed many times. His assassin, Sir Robert Graham, is said to have screamed: 'I have slain and delivered you of so cruel a tyrant, the greatest enemy that Scotland might have.'

Look out – it gets worse...

Robert Graham escaped but was found hiding beneath a rock on the edge of Loch Bhac, still known as Graham's Rock. He was captured and carried naked through the streets of Edinburgh in a cart, with his hand nailed to a post while being poked with sharp hooks and red-hot irons. The following day he was forced to watch his son being disembowelled alive before suffering the same fate himself. Then his body was cut into quarters, just to make certain. Yuk. Moral of the story: try not to kill the King of Scotland.

Mary, Queen of Scots

1542-1587

(A sad and gruesome story)

> Och, this bit is a pain in the neck

Queen Mary was born when Henry VIII was King of England. Her father was King James V of Scotland but he died when she was a baby. Although Mary became Queen of Scotland, she lived in France as a girl and married the king of France – Francis II. She was fifteen and he was fourteen but he died two years after they married.

Back in Scotland, Mary later married her cousin, Lord Darnley. He was very unpopular with the people of Scotland as he was violent and bad-tempered. He hated Mary's secretary (an Italian called David Rizzio). While Mary was entertaining friends in her private rooms, Darnley and his gang stabbed Rizzio over 50 times, killing him in front of her. Mary was horrified – but she planned revenge.

Shortly after their son James was born, Mary and Darnley were staying near Edinburgh. Late in the evening Mary rode off to visit friends. Scotland was a very dangerous country in the Sixteenth Century and it was risky to be out at night. Maybe she knew the house they were staying in was about to be blown up. Darnley's body was found in the garden of the house. The explosion hadn't killed him – he'd been strangled. Fishy!

Hi, I'm Prince James (to become King of Scotland AND of England)

Just three months later, Mary married Bothwell. He was as disliked as Darnley, so many Scots plotted against Mary. She was arrested and held prisoner at Lochleven Castle. Mary didn't help herself. She made it clear she should be the Queen of England, instead of Elizabeth I (her cousin). It's never wise to upset your cousin. Queen Elizabeth signed a death warrant, so in 1587 Mary was led to the chopping block.

CROSS ALERT

Mary was blindfolded as she knelt on a velvet cushion and rested her head on the wooden block. The axe was raised, all gasped and... THWACK. Oops. What should have taken a single stroke of the axe needed a lot of retakes. Ouch. The first strike hit the back of her head – and some in the crowd saw Mary's lips move. The second thwack severed most of her neck, but it took one final chop to complete the job.

Hair today, gone tomorrow!

The executioner held Mary's head up and shouted, 'God save the Queen!' Oops again. He was left holding her wig as her head fell and rolled across the floor. Apparently, Mary's small terrier dog had been hiding in her skirts during the whole ghastly execution, and it refused to leave its dead owner. It was covered in blood and had to be dragged off and given a good wash. All very messy.

Mary's son (now king of England) later buried his mother's body in a grand tomb in London, at Westminster Abbey. Her dog probably ended up living happily in France.

Call me 'scentimental', but I want to be called 'your highness'.

King Pong

Queen Mary's son was King James VI of Scotland (James I of England) but he was a bit of a stinker. He didn't have a lot of time for personal hygiene. Although the king, he wore the same clothes for months on end, even sleeping in them now and again. He also kept the same hat on 24/7 until it rotted to a frazzle. He refused to wash or bath as he was convinced it was bad for his health. Wrong, your HIGHness (no doubt smelling to HIGH heaven).

ANOTHER FAMOUS SCOT YOU MIGHT SEE ON TINS OF SHORTBREAD OR TOURISTS' T-SHIRTS...

Bonnie Prince Charlie
1720-1788

Troubles between Scotland and England rumbled on. The different royal families were forever squabbling. Charles was the grandson of James VII of Scotland (James II of England) and known as Bonnie Prince Charlie. He refused to be ruled by King George II of England so came up with a plan. He led the last major push for Scottish independence which became known as the Jacobite rebellion.

Fast facts:

1 The word Jacobite comes from the Latin for his grandfather's name – James. In Latin James is Jacobus.

2 Bonnie Prince Charlie grew up in Italy and he had never been to Scotland until he started the Scottish uprising when he was 25.

I'm looking for Bonnie Prince Charlie's bucket list

3 He led his army to defeat at the Battle of Culloden in 1746. In fact, the battle wasn't so much Scotland versus England as Scotland versus Scotland as there were more Scots in the army that defeated Bonnie Prince Charlie than there were in his own army. So, although a popular character, Bonnie Prince Charlie failed to help Scotland.

4 After his defeat, Bonnie Prince Charlie went back to live in Italy, where he died in Rome at the age of 68.

Bonnie Prince Charlie ran and hid, just like a rat playing 'hide and squeak'

A Bonnie Wee Joke

Teacher to class: 'Right class, today is Thursday so we're going to have a quiz. The pupil who gets the answer right can have Friday off and not come back until Tuesday. Who can tell me who said: "Don't ask what your country can do for you , but what you can do for your country"?'

Wee Jimmy shoots up his hand but the teacher chooses Morag. 'Yes, Morag?'

Morag (sounding very posh): 'The answer is J F Kennedy in 1960, miss.'

Teacher: 'Very good, Morag. You may come back on Tuesday. Next question. Who said. "We will fight them on the beaches, we will fight them in the air, we will fight them at sea. But we will never surrender"?'

Wee Jimmy shoots up his hand, shouting, 'I know!' but the teacher chooses Andrew.

Andrew answers in an even posher English accent: 'The answer is Winston Churchill, 1941, Battle of Britain speech, miss.'

'Very good, Andrew. You may come back on Tuesday. Last question. Who said: "tell our enemies that they may take our lives, but they'll never take... OUR FREEDOM"?'

Wee Jimmy jumps up and down with both hands up, yelling 'I know!'

Pay attention, wee Jimmy laddie

The teacher asks Prudence, who answers in a frightfully plummy English accent: 'William Wallace in the 1995 film *Braveheart*.'

'Very good, Prudence, you may come back on Tuesday.'

Wee Jimmy blurts out, 'Wherever did all these stuck-up English toffs come from?'

Teacher (looking round the class): 'Who said that?'

Wee Jimmy: 'Bonnie Prince Charlie, Culloden, 1746. See ya Tuesday!'

FOLKLORE, FACT AND FICTION
– there's nothing quite like a fine old Scottish Yarn

The Eagle and the Baby

A 300-year-old story may well make you sob into your porridge.

A Scottish crofter called William Anderson lived on the island of Unst. He and his wife were cutting hay, while their young baby, Mary, slept at the edge of the field. As they worked further up the field, the parents heard a strange noise behind them. They looked back in horror to see a large sea-eagle swooping down, clutching their baby and shawl in its talons, then flying off with her.

The shocked parents and neighbours ran
after the bird but could only watch helplessly
as it swept out over the sea towards the
nearby island of Fetlar.
They rushed to find a small fishing boat and
rowed out to Fetlar where locals told them
there was a sea-eagle's nest on the high cliffs.

What do you call a sick bird of prey that steals a baby?

Grabbing ropes, they set off to the high, craggy rocks – where a 12-year-old boy called Robert Nicholson offered to climb the jagged cliffs to the nest. When he finally reached it, he found the baby unharmed and still wrapped in her shawl, lying between two eaglets. The mother eagle had flown off again, so Robert was able to scoop up baby Mary in one arm then scramble away over the rocks with her.

Yes, you've guessed (get ready to cry), years later when Mary grew up, she married her rescuer. Robert and Mary were said to live happily ever after – with their descendants still living on Shetland today. They are known as 'Eagle Bairns' to this day. Don't you think this legend would make a great musical?

Ill eagle!

DeaCon Brodie

A notorious Scotsman has gone down in history for leading a sinister double life. William Brodie (1741-88) was a skilful cabinet-maker and a member of Edinburgh's Town Council. But behind this respectable image, Brodie was a secret night-time leader of a gang of burglars. He had the perfect day job for his crimes, as he made and repaired locks. This was ideal when he worked on the locks of his wealthy customers' houses. By copying their door-keys, he could return with his gang at night and steal all sorts. No one had a clue that the trustworthy Deacon Brodie turned into a greedy villain after dark.

Brodie's last crime was an armed raid on His Majesty's Excise Office but two of his gang got caught and told the authorities everything. Brodie escaped to the Netherlands but was arrested and returned to Edinburgh for trial in 1788.

The jury found Brodie guilty and his execution was set – a public hanging. But Brodie had another plan and bribed the hangman to ignore a steel collar he'd wear to protect his throat from the noose. He arranged for his 'body' to be quickly removed after the hanging so he could be revived.

Oops, his plan didn't work and he was successfully hanged in front of a jeering crowd of 40,000. Funnily enough (but not for him) Brodie was hanged from gallows which he had recently redesigned himself. He proudly boasted to the crowd that this gallows was the most efficient of its kind ever. Correct!

I won't be hanging around much longer

Dodgy Doctors

Edinburgh has been a major centre for science, education and medicine for centuries. Scotland has produced many great doctors and surgeons. Some were famous for a few foul facts...

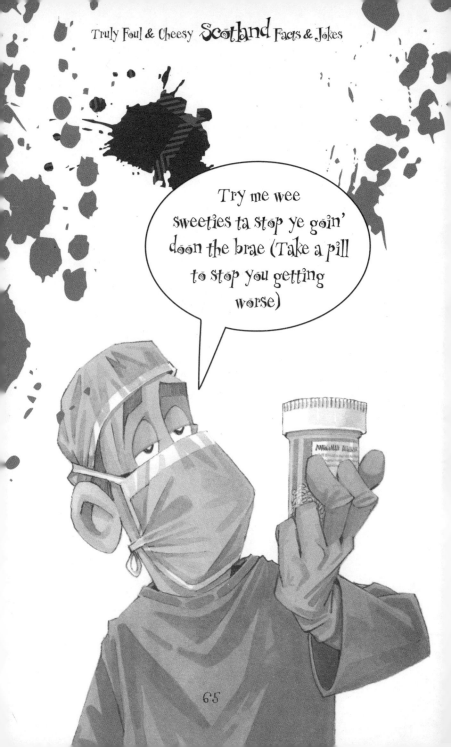

Robert Liston
(1794 to 1847)

Liston was a pioneering Scottish surgeon, often described as the best of his time (particularly by himself!). In an age before anaesthetics, surgery was very dangerous. Operations had to be fast if a patient was to have any chance of surviving. Robert Liston was one of the best surgeons in Scotland because he was recorded cutting off a leg and stitching the wound in just 28 seconds. He often boasted about his speed and he made enemies who didn't like the way he performed his operations in front of admiring audiences.

In 1846 Liston became the first surgeon in Europe to use ether as an anaesthetic during an operation. Because he was something of a show-off, he wasn't too popular in Scotland and stories were told of his mistakes.

In one operation to remove a leg, while a team of helpers held the patient down, Liston moved so fast that he cut off his assistant's fingers and slashed a spectator's coat. The patient and the assistant both died from infections to their wounds, and the spectator was so scared that he died of shock. Whether entirely true or not, one thing was certain – it was bad news if you had to meet the feared Robert Liston on the operating table. Even though he was a good surgeon and told everyone so, your chances of surviving his knife weren't too great.

No need to rush – I'm reading the sports results.

Robert Knox (1791 to 1862)

was also a surgeon in Edinburgh but he had to escape to London when his reputation was ruined. In 1826, Robert Knox became principal of the successful Barclay's Anatomy School in Surgeon's Square. At the time, the study of anatomy had a problem: the only dead bodies available to study came from executed prisoners. There weren't enough to go around, so body-snatching teams known as 'resurrectionists' dug up graves and sold corpses to medical schools. Robert Knox's downfall came through the foul activities of two men called Burke and Hare, who went further than bodysnatching. They killed people and delivered the bodies to Knox. In 1827, Knox paid £7 for their first body, then up to £15 if bodies were 'fresh'. Burke and Hare murdered 17 people before being caught.

Knox was never prosecuted for his part in the murders and he became so despised that he eventually moved to London to restart his career. He had to go alone as he had NO BODY left to go with!

Children at the time would sing a rhyme about the whole grisly story:

Knox was the butcher
who bought the beef.
Burke was the butcher,
Hare was the thief.

GROSS ALERT...

You can still glimpse some of William Burke today. After he was hanged, grisly souvenirs started to appear – with books and wallets made from his skin being sold on the streets. A pocket book made from Burke's skin is on display at Surgeons' Hall Museum in Edinburgh. But it's best not to judge a book by its cover!

EXTRA
GROSS
ALERT...

After Matthew Clydesdale was hanged
for murder in 1818, his body was taken to
Glasgow University where Professor Jeffray
demonstrated to his audience how an electric
shock could make a body move. To the
horror of the professor and his students, the
corpse suddenly shot up and pointed a finger
at the screaming onlookers. **SHOCKING!**

Shaggy Dog Story
(TO MAKE YOU CRY)

You may know the famous tale (or tail?) of Greyfriars
Bobby. He was a small Skye Terrier who was devoted
to his owner, known as Auld Jock Gray. They went
everywhere together but sadly Jock died in 1858 and his
body was buried in Greyfriars kirkyard in Edinburgh.
It was strictly out of bounds to dogs, but Bobby was
determined never to leave his master. Although they
tried to drive Bobby away, he was eventually allowed
to sleep by his master's grave. Bobby spent 14 years at
Greyfriars, where he became famous and thousands
came to see him, including Queen Victoria.

Shooing Bobby
away was a grave
mistake

72

Bobby died in 1872 when he was 16 years old. His grave is not far from his master's. On the headstone, it says:

Greyfriars Bobby –
died 14th January 1872.
Let his loyalty be a
lesson to us all.

You can see the statue of Bobby at Greyfriars today. Tourists sobbing into tissues like to rub his nose to bring them good luck (even though they probably spread all kinds of germs!).

Talking of tourists...

With all its stunning scenery, mountains, lochs, islands, ancient castles and cities, Scotland has millions of visitors every year from all over the world.

Honey, was that a cat being strangled or the sound of bagpipes?

Landlady:	Welcome to our fine old Scottish Castle.
American Visitor:	It feels real draughty with no glass in the windows.
Landlady:	It's our special Scottish air conditioning.
American Visitor:	I hope you've got running water in all rooms.
Landlady:	Och, of course. Mainly down the walls.
American Visitor:	I can't believe it's so cold and wet here. When's your summer?
Landlady:	It was last Tuesday.
American Visitor:	Are your guests woken in the morning by a Scottish piper?
Landlady:	Yes. If you're not up by six thirty, my husband will hit you round the head with his bagpipes. If we like you, we'll serve you a wee haggis for breakfast.
American Visitor:	And if you don't like me?

Landlady: You'll get two big haggises.

American Visitor: I see you've got tartan carpet and curtains everywhere.

Landlady: Yes, we wanted tartan walls but we ran out of tartan paint.

American Visitor: It looks as if your eyes are tartan, too.

Landlady: That's right – I've just had them checked.

American Visitor: I think I met you last time I was in Scotland. I'm sure I've seen your face somewhere else.

Landlady: Och no, it's always been on the front of my head.

American Visitor: But I've got a very good memory for faces.

Landlady: That's good because there's no mirror in the bathroom.

American Visitor: How much land do you have here?

Landlady: Just a few acres.

American Visitor: Gee, that's nothing. Back home it takes me all day to drive around all my ranch.

Landlady: Aye, I once had a rubbish American car, too. You might see a fine Scottish stag on our land.

American Visitor: That's nothing. Back home I hunt for moose.

Landlady: How big is a moose?

American Visitor: It's over two metres tall.

Landlady: Och, if that's a moose, I'd hate to see one of your rats!

There's a moose loose aboot this hoose.

More Limericks

In a bleak Scottish castle, the host
Said, 'To all my ancestors, a toast!'
Doors swung with a burst,
All the crowd feared the worst...
A gust! A guest aghast! You've
guessed – a GHOST!

A fisherman thief on the Clyde,
Cooked salmon but not baked or fried.
When asked to say why,
It's just because I
Am a poacher by trade', he replied.

SO MUCH FOR DAFT LIMERICKS.
Real Scottish poetry needs the famous Bard of Scotland...

Robert Burns
1759 – 1796

Robert Burns (aka Rabbie Burns) was born on 25th January 1759 in Ayrshire, Scotland. Today Burns Night is celebrated on that date every year in Scotland and all over the world.

He wrote his poems in Scots, standard English and Scots dialect.

He was a brilliant lyricist and he contributed over 100 songs to a book called *The Melodies of Scotland*. He also wrote lyrics for *A Select Collection of Scottish Airs for the Voice* and The Scots Musical Museum. He also wrote 'Auld Lang Syne' (meaning 'times long past' – adding new lyrics to a traditional Scottish tune).

Robert Burns died at the age of 37. His body lies in the Burns Mausoleum in Dumfries.

Robert Burns has been voted 'The Greatest Scot'. He beat William Wallace, Sir Alexander Fleming and Robert the Bruce.

Auld Lang Syne

I know a man, old Mr Lang
Whose window has a sign.
'Cheers New Year'
it says in slang.
They call it Old Lang's Sign.
(Get it?)

ANOTHER bad joke

A new doctor goes into a Scottish hospital to meet the patients. As he's being taken around one of the wards, a patient shouts, 'Wee cowerin' timorous beastie.'
The doctor backs away to the next bed where another patient shouts, 'You take the high road and I'll take the low road and I'll be in Scotland afore ye!'
The doctor hurries to the next bed where another patient sings 'On the bonnie banks of Loch Lomond' followed by 'Get down South you Sassenachs!'

Suddenly the whole ward chants, 'Wahay the Scots and Bonnie Prince Charlie and Rabbie the Baird and the Lord of the Isles!' The doctor turns to a nurse and asks 'Why are they all spouting Scottish poetry – are they mad?'

'No,' says the nurse, 'this is the Serious Burns Unit!'

Try this wee toddy as a cure for cheesy jokes

The land of
GENIUS

SCOTLAND IS THE LAND OF INVENTIONS AND DISCOVERY. DID YOU KNOW THESE 3 FAMOUS SCOTSMEN CALLED ALEXANDER CHANGED THE WORLD?

No 'Foul & Cheesy Book' would be complete without a toilet so here GOES...

1 Alexander Cummings designed the flushing toilet. In 1775 he invented the, S-trap – still in use today – which uses standing water to prevent nasty smells backing up out of the sewer.

2 Alexander Graham Bell invented the telephone in Boston in February 1876.

3 Alexander Fleming was a scientist best known for his Nobel Prize-winning discovery of the antibiotic penicillin in 1928.

I do enjoy Scottish culture

Scotland has also given to the world all of these everyday things (although you'd have to have an exciting life to use them all in one day): adhesive stamps, bicycle pedals, Bovril, chloroform, colour photography, the Encyclopaedia Britannica, the fountain pen, fingerprinting, the hypodermic syringe, the lawnmower, lime cordial, the MRI scanner, postmarks, the pneumatic tyre, radar, savings banks, the speedometer, the raincoat, Tarmac, the vacuum flask and even chicken tikka masala, which was invented in Glasgow in the late 1960s. And don't forget it was a Scotsman, John Logie Baird, who created the world's first TV picture in October 1925. And to think, he didn't have to go to a commercial break.

Scottish Women

Never think Scotland is just about Scotsmen. Scotswomen have also changed the world, particularly in education, science and medicine. Thanks to 'The Edinburgh Seven' (Sophia, Isabel, Edith, Matilda, Helen, Mary and Emily), things would never be the same again.

Baaa!

These young women were the first female students ever to study at a British university. They enrolled at Edinburgh University to study medicine in 1869, but male students were appalled and organised a mob to stop them taking their exams. The 'Surgeons' Hall Riot' involved letting a sheep loose in the exam room. A baaaaad thing to do and the authorities wouldn't stop BLEATING on about it, so they didn't let the women graduate from Edinburgh University. However, their campaign eventually changed the law to allow women to qualify as doctors in the UK and Ireland. At last.

The Loch Ness Monster

THE MOST FAMOUS SCOT OF ALL TIME?

6 FUN FACTS ABOUT NESSIE THE BEASTIE:

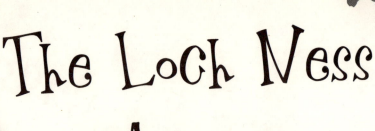

1 Loch Ness contains more water than all the lakes of England and Wales combined – but it's not Scotland's biggest Loch (that's Loch Lomond).

2 The chilly water is only 6 degrees Celsius all year round. Even in winter Loch Ness never freezes over and on very cold winter days you can see steam rising from the surface of the Loch, as it is warmer than the surrounding air. Ideal for a wallowing monster.

3 The waters of Loch Ness are very dark due to the peat washed from the hills into the Loch – perfect cover for any creatures that might be living in the depths.

4 The first ever Nessie sighting was way back in **565 AD** by St Columba. According to legend, the Irish monk's servant was attacked by a 'water beast', although the attack is said to have happened on the **River Ness** rather than the Loch itself.

AHHH!

5 Today you can use Google Earth to look for Nessie under the surface of the Loch.

6 70 miles from Loch Ness another humped serpent-like creature is said to be Nessie's cousin. She is Morag, the monster of Loch Morar – the deepest freshwater lake in the British Isles, with a maximum depth of 310 metres. The first recorded sighting of Morag was in 1887.

Limerick of the Loch

If you stand on the shores
of Loch Ness
With your swimwear and
start to undress,
There might be eyes peeping
From submerged beasties
creeping...
And what might come
next... you can guess!

Ridiculous Riddles

Q: What's fifty metres long, scary
and sings 'Scotland The Brave'?
A: The Loch Ness Songster.

Q: What did one highland
cow say to the other?
A: Och aye the moo.

Q: Which famous Scottish poet is really setting the world on fire?
A: Robbie Burns.

Q: Why is a Scottish boy with a cold like a Scottish girl at Half Term?
A: They both have a wee cough (week off).

Q: What do you call a Scottish creature that hangs people?
A: The Loch Noose Monster.

Q: What's cold, stripy, moves around the loch and is sometimes heard at weird times?
A: The Loch Ness ice cream van.

Scotland–
THE LAND OF POETRY

Many events from Scotland's tragic past were recorded in poems.

This is just the first verse of The Tay Bridge Disaster in 1880 by the Scottish poet William McGonagall. He wasn't quite as good as Robert Burns and even changed the number of people killed in the train crash just to make it fit his first verse...

Beautiful Railway Bridge of
the Silv'ry Tay!
Alas! I am very sorry to say
That ninety lives have been
taken away
On the last Sabbath day of 1879,
Which will be remember'd for
a very long time.

The actual number of people killed when the bridge collapsed in a winter storm, plunging the six carriages of the Dundee train to their fate, was more likely 75. The Bridge spanned two miles across the firth of Tay, making it the longest bridge in the world at the time it was built – when Queen Victoria travelled across it. A new bridge was completed within five years and opened in 1887.

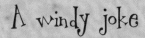

A windy joke

Mrs MacTavish went to the doctor, complaining of strange noises from her 'down below'.

After a quick listen with a stethoscope, the doctor said, 'You've just been eating too many neeps and tatties – it's nothing more than a wee bit of wind. There's no harm with a wee bit of wind now and again.'

'No harm with a wee bit of wind?' Mrs MacTavish snapped. 'Have ye ne'er heard what it did to the Tay Bridge? I demand you give me something right noo for "a wee bit of wind".'

'Very well, Mrs MacTavish. I'll write you a wee prescription... for a kite.'

Q: When can you tell if a Scotsman is a true gentleman?
A: When, even though he can play the bagpipes, he doesn't.

Spooky Lighthouse Mystery

Of all the Scottish islands, Eilean Mòr is among the most mysterious. It was always said to be haunted by dead sailors lost in its dangerous waters.

Flannan Isles Lighthouse is 15 miles west of the Isle of Lewis, near the highest point on Eilean Mòr. This is the Outer Hebrides off the west coast of Scotland. The lighthouse is still remembered for the mysterious disappearance of its keepers in 1900. A poem by Wilfrid Wilson Gibson (1878–1962) tells the tragic tale. The first verse goes…

Though three men dwell on
Flannan Isle
To keep the lamp alight,
As we steered under the lee,
we caught
No glimmer through the night.

On Boxing Day, 1900, a supply boat called at the new lighthouse, just as it did every two weeks. It brought food and picked up one of the lighthouse keepers for his leave. Three men lived and worked in the lighthouse as its light wasn't automatic then. But something was wrong. There was no sign of life on the small island. There was no flag flying and no empty boxes on the jetty.

The landing party entered the deserted lighthouse. The clock had stopped, the fire was out and the three men who should have been on duty were missing. There were no signs of violence, the main room was tidy and food was in the cupboards. Everything seemed as it should be, although no oilskins were hanging up. That was odd because all three men would never go outside at the same time.

A bad storm had struck two weeks before. The log for 12th December said: 'Waves very high. Tearing at lighthouse. Storm still raging, cannot go out.'

The last entry in the log was 3 days later on 15th December. '1pm. Storm ended, sea calm. God is over all.......' No more was to be heard from the three lighthouse keepers. They were never seen again.

With Scotland being steeped in mysteries, myths and superstitions, some said the men had been turned into crows by an ancient curse. Others told strange tales of skeleton pirates carrying them away. Scotland is well-known for UFO sightings – did aliens carry off the men? Or maybe a freak wave washed them all away. We will never know the answer.

Loopy Limericks

A hen on the small Isle of Eigg
(And you might think I'm pulling
your leigg)
Fell in love with a pig
At a Scottish farm jig
And laid the first ever Scotch Eigg!

What a lot of hogwash

A man from the Island of Bute
Always dressed in a fine tartan suit
But a thread of his tweed
Unravelled at speed...
In a flash, he was nude as a coot!

A lady from Leith, Miss McWarren,
Avoided all men who were foreign.
She only had time
For a Scot in his prime
In kilt, tam o' shanter and sporran.

I like snappy limericks

A rather wee lass from Argyll
Is known for her very sweet smile
But the thing about Julia
Is her looks will soon fool-yer
As she snaps like a mad crocodile!

There was a young girl of Dundee
Who liked to drink cups of hot tea.
When poured scotch broth instead,
She got all upset
And said she didn't see the point of
limericks in the first place.

Scottish Symbols

Knock. Knock.
Who's there?
Thistle
Thistle who?
Thistle be the third time I've told
you what the emblem of Scotland is.

Knock. Knock.
Who's there?
Unique
Unique who?
Unicorns are Scotland's national
animal on its coat of arms.

Q: What is the difference
between a unicorn and a carrot?
A: One is a funny beast and the
other is a bunny feast.

106

I have a unique horn

Unicorn

A mythical creature may seem an odd choice for a country's national animal, but a unicorn has been a Scottish heraldic symbol since the 12th century, when it was used on the Scottish coat of arms by William I (unless it was a horse with a traffic cone stuck on its head).

AND FINALLY...

MORE SCOTTISH INVENTIONS

Hallowe'en

The word (from All Hallows' Evening) is Scottish in origin – arising out of ancient Celtic celebrations of Samhain ('summer's end') that signalled the end of the harvest season. Some Scots would leave an empty chair and a plate of food – believing that ghosts would come out on Hallowe'en. How ghoulies and ghosties love a free haggis.

Long John Silver

Shiver me timbers, the meanest, nastiest pirate on the high seas was dreamt up by Edinburgh-born *Treasure Island* author Robert Louis Stevenson. With a parrot on his shoulder and a wooden leg, Long John Silver became the image of scary swashbuckling pirates around the world, ooo arrrrrh, me hearties.

Scotland's links to pirates go beyond stories, though. Captain Kidd, executed in 1701 for piracy, was born in Dundee.

Golf Caddy

In golf, that great Scottish sport, a caddy (or caddie) is the person who carries a player's bag and clubs. When Mary, Queen of Scots went to France as a young girl, the King of France knew that she liked to play golf so he had the first course outside of Scotland made for her.

To make sure she was properly looked after while she played, the king hired cadets from a military school to accompany her. When Mary returned to Scotland (not the best move as it turned out), she took the idea with her. In French, the word cadet is pronounced 'ca-day' and the Scots changed it into 'caddie'. So now you know where the idea of caddies came from.

I'm carrying another pair of pants in case she gets a hole in one.

111

Place names

A village near Dumfries and Galloway has the shortest place name in the UK. The name of the village is Ae. At least that's easier to say and spell than another town in Dumfries and Galloway – which sounds like a short coughing fit. Here goes: Ecclefechan

How about this place?

Auchtermuchty

In Gaelic, this Fife town means 'high ground of the pig rearing'.

SQUAWK!

3 last jokes

Other brands of burger are available - I've tried them all.

Did you hear about the American tourists who stopped off at a burger bar in Milngavie in East Dunbartonshire and wondered how the name was pronounced? They thought they'd find out from a local so they asked the waitress: 'Can you tell us how you pronounce the name of this place and say it slowly so that we can pick it up?'
The lass smiled and said very slowly and clearly, 'B-u-r-g-e-r K-i-n-g'.
(By the way, it's actually pronounced 'Mill-guy'.)

2 'How's the flat you're living in down there in London, dear?' asks Jimmy's mother when he calls home to Aberdeen.

'It's okay,' he replies, 'but the woman next door keeps screaming and crying all night and the guy on the other side keeps banging his head on the wall.'

'Never you mind,' says his mother, 'don't you let them get to you, just ignore them.'

'Aye, that I do,' he says, 'I don't say a word. I just carry on playing my bagpipes.'

Why do bagpipers walk when they play? To get away from the row!

114

Time to spin a wee yarn

3

Once upon a time, a poor girl had to spin straw into gold for the King of Scotland but she had no idea how to go about it. Suddenly a wee Scotsman half her size appeared and began spinning bales of straw into the finest gold. 'You must tell me your name,' the girl said. 'You'll never guess it,' the little man replied, sitting on a straw bale in his kilt (whatever was he doing with a straw bale in his kilt?) 'Then let me give you a name,' the girl smiled, as the wee Scotsman scratched madly at all the straw caught under his kilt, chafing his legs and causing a lumpy rash on his bottom. She giggled, 'I shall call you Rumpled Kilt Skin!'

FAVOURITE ONE-LINER JOKES FROM

The Edinburgh Festival Fringe

'My gran hates her new stair lift. She says it drives her up the wall.'

'I just deleted all the German names off my phone. Now it's Hans free.'

'I think a body's buried in my allotment. There's twice as much soil as the week before. It's a real mystery. The plot thickens.'

Final Teaser

What do you think these are: Blue Murder, Baby Bonnet, Biggar Blue, Cambus O' May, Loch Arthur, Strathdon Blue, Arran Blue? How could we finish a 'foul and cheesy' book without a hefty chunk of Dunlop Cheddar and other Scottish cheeses? Yes, tasty cheese-making in Scotland is far from a cheesy joke!

QUIZ

1. Who first brought bagpipes to Scotland?

a) The Romans

b) The Gloamins

c) Aliens

2. What language did the ancient Celts speak?

a) Garlic

b) Gaelic

c) Gaulic

3. What is the highest mountain in Scotland?

a) Ben Fogle

b) Ben Stiller

c) Ben Nevis

4. What is traditional haggis made from?

a) Scottish kippers

b) Sheep's liver

c) Deep-fried Mars Bars

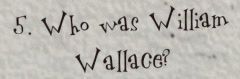

5. Who was William Wallace?

a) A Scottish freedom fighter

b) A Scottish haggis-maker

c) A Scottish writer

6. Who was the son of Mary, Queen of Scots?

a) James MacDonald

b) Jimmy Riddle

c) James VI

7. What happened to Mary, Queen of Scots?

a) She defeated the English at the Battle of Neasden

b) She led an army up Ben Nevis with an elephant

c) She lost her head

8. For what has Edinburgh been a centre for a long time?

a) Science and medicine

b) Haggis growing

c) Many styles of tartan paint

9. Who was Greyfriars Bobby?

a) A friendly policeman in Glasgow

b) A small dog in Edinburgh

c) A famous surgeon in Dundee

10. What is the famous pirate story by Scottish writer Robert Louis Stevenson?

a) Treasure Island

b) Pie Rats of the Caribbean

c) Silver Long Johns

Answers:
1 = a
2 = b
3 = c
4 = b
5 = a
6 = c
7 = c
8 = a
9 = b
10 = a

GLOSSARY

Anatomy the study of the human body and those of other living organisms

Bard a writer skilled at composing and presenting dramatic verses

Chloroform a colourless liquid previously used as an anaesthetic

Deacon a leader in a church or guild

Disembowel to cut open a body and remove the internal organs

Hogmanay the name for New Year celebrations in Scotland (Gaelic for 'new morning')

Loch a Scottish lake or an arm of the sea surrounded by land

INDEX

I finished reading this Truly
Foul & Cheesy book on:

........../........../..........